ITALY TODAY

ITALY
today

Photographs by Karol Kállay

ARTIA

Designed by Karol Kállay
© 1963 by Artia Prague
Printed in Czechoslovakia
S 1486

KAROL KÁLLAY has presented an original and striking picture of Italy today in this collection of realistic photographs. On a brief visit during the summer months he used his camera to record arresting facets of the towns he visited.

He caught the country off-guard, and found it a land of paradox. The old and the new, affluence and squalor, art and artifice, are captured uncomfortably side by side. An often irregular pulse of changing ideas and new concepts throbs in the veins of the modern Italian.

For this volatile, quick-witted, practical people is not content to bask in the glory of its mediaeval history.

Since the Risorgimento and the strife of the 19th century, Italy has taken great strides forward in her position in Western Europe. Two World Wars have only put a temporary brake on the development of her resources.

D'Szeglio, Prime Minister of Piedmont, and forerunner of the political genius, Cavour, said:
'We have made Italy. We have now to make Italians.'

He realised that the process of unification would be a slow one: that a country with such an enormous range of geographical diversities, considering its comparatively small territory, would find difficulty in establishing a national character, and combining in common ideals.

The Alps sweep across the north forming a natural border of snow-capped towers. The Apennine Chain invades the whole length of the land. The River Po, springing from the Cottian Alps, flows through four hundred miles of fertile plain and valley to the Adriatic Sea. There are the deep blue Lombard Lakes, their shores clothed with cyprus and palm trees and, to the east, the vast sandy beaches lining the cost of Liguria.

Wooded mountain slopes jut ruggedly up to the sky to make the wild and savage country of the Vulture in the Basilicata, a waste land of 'macchia' where only aromatic herbs, cork-oak, and other Mediterranean type vegetation can withstand the long summer drought. And in Sicily, Mount Aetna towers over remote and bare knots of mountains, looking south to the African shore.

All this is Italy.

The isolation and resultant poverty of southern and central Italy is now being dramatically tackled by the government. The Cassa del Mezzogiorno — an organisation to promote economic progress in these areas — is working hard to reclaim land, and teach the local inhabitants new agricultural and industrial techniques.

Slowly, a levelling of living conditions and standards is being brought about between the naturally rich north and the poorer south. It is only the visitor who will regret the decay of the primitive but picturesque village on the mountainside, and the passing of the tiny, olive-growing smallholdings that can no longer support their sons. A generation of eager, dark-eyed children is emerging, no longer content to scratch a living from the soil. They can read and write, and even their parents, educated by the Scuole de Populari — an educational organisation particularly for adults — are looking ahead.

Despite this process, there remains a great regional pride and diversity in mode of living. Every area is rich in folk-lore and traditions fostered by its own historical background. Old customs and festivals survive, indicating perhaps that although the people are intensely aware of the future and its problems, they are also proud to remember their past.

And the past, to Italians, is synonymous with Catholicism. Ever since the Emperor Constantine pronounced Christianity to be the national faith, Rome has been the centre for believers all over the world. The Pope, in the magnificence of the palaces of the Vatican, reigns over the spiritual life of the country, and to some extent, through the offices of his Archbishops and Bishops, holds much temporal power to this day.

With striking insight, Kallay has spotlighted two women. The one hesitates over the price of a bottle of wine, and the other presides over a candle stall, the price of each candle — the value of a prayer.

This warmth, this faith, is an inherent part of Italy today as it was yesterday.

In every town, a proud church or 'duomo' stands, built of lasting stone and faced with marble — the white marble from Carrara and Lucca, the coloured, from Verona, Vicenza or Porto Venere —

and life revolves around it. Even gatherings of citizens to discuss political or local problems have often been held within the portals of the churches or the Piazza Communale outside.

For, first and foremost, the Italians are an urban people, a way of life initiated by their Roman ancestors. A 'landed gentry', as such, never existed, for the land-owners were always town dwellers while armies of dispossessed peasants farmed their acres for them. Hence the great beauty of their cities.

A cultural heritage of over three thousand years gives these cities a bewildering number of schools and periods of style in architecture, sculpture, and painting. The scenery and climate seem to have fostered pioneers of new art forms that have since formed the basis of Western Art.

Thus, Italy is the centre of Classical, Mediaeval, Renaissance, and Baroque periods of activity: the Greek colonists left the purity of the Doric form; the Etruscans, their constructional ideas in decoration and bronze sculpture; the Romans, arches, vaults, palaces, and the first churches in Europe; the Byzantine period embellishing Roman buildings with domes and minarets. Then came the Cistercian monks who introduced the Gothic art form and the aerial palaces of Venice, and later, a revolution in sculpture and painting by Pisano and Giotto. The Renaissance followed with the building of the vast Basilica of St Peter's in Rome, and the work of Leonardo da Vinci, Michelangelo, and Raphael. Finally, came the Baroque period, an irrational and instinctive art form led by Bernini, Borromini and Caravaggio.

Today, Italy finds different fields to conquer. During the tumult of the 19th century, her genius lay idle, but is being rediscovered in the world of fashion and cinema productions.

Kállay offers us glimpses of this new Italy, both of its riches and its poverty. He has seen and recorded what the endless troops of tourists could easily miss. Clutching their guide books they stare at the immense displays of architecture and sculpture, but a gnarled priest hurries by with his eyes on the ground, a gondolier lounges while he waits for trade, men gossip, and the children chalk games on the wall or shyly hug their treasures.

Advertisements, and more advertisements, share the scene. They mix incongruously with a haloed saint against a Roman skyline, and mock the walls of a canal in Venice.

Tram-wires cut across the rounded dome of the Santa Maria del Fiore.

A shack is propped against a streamlined skyscraper.

It is these things that the visitor busily 'doing' the masterpieces in the Uffizi Gallery, or photographing friends in locally-purchased straw hats against a backcloth of cathedral or fountain, may never notice.

For Italy moves forward with the rest of the world, and to make way for the new, much of the old must be sacrificed. Rome, particularly, has shed much of her former peace and contemplative atmosphere. The hum of traffic shakes at the foundations of her palazzi, silent and guarded though they are within. The statue of Romulus and Remus feeding from their she-wolf foster mother looks out now, not only over ancient and Renaissance Rome, but over new and spreading suburbs of modern white villas overflowing into the pine-scented hills of Lazio.

Anachronisms or virtues, these things are the work of a living, growing people, and could be seen as more refreshing than disturbing. The 'Garden of Europe' remains, but as D'Azeglio foresaw, the ebullient Italians are still in the making.

9

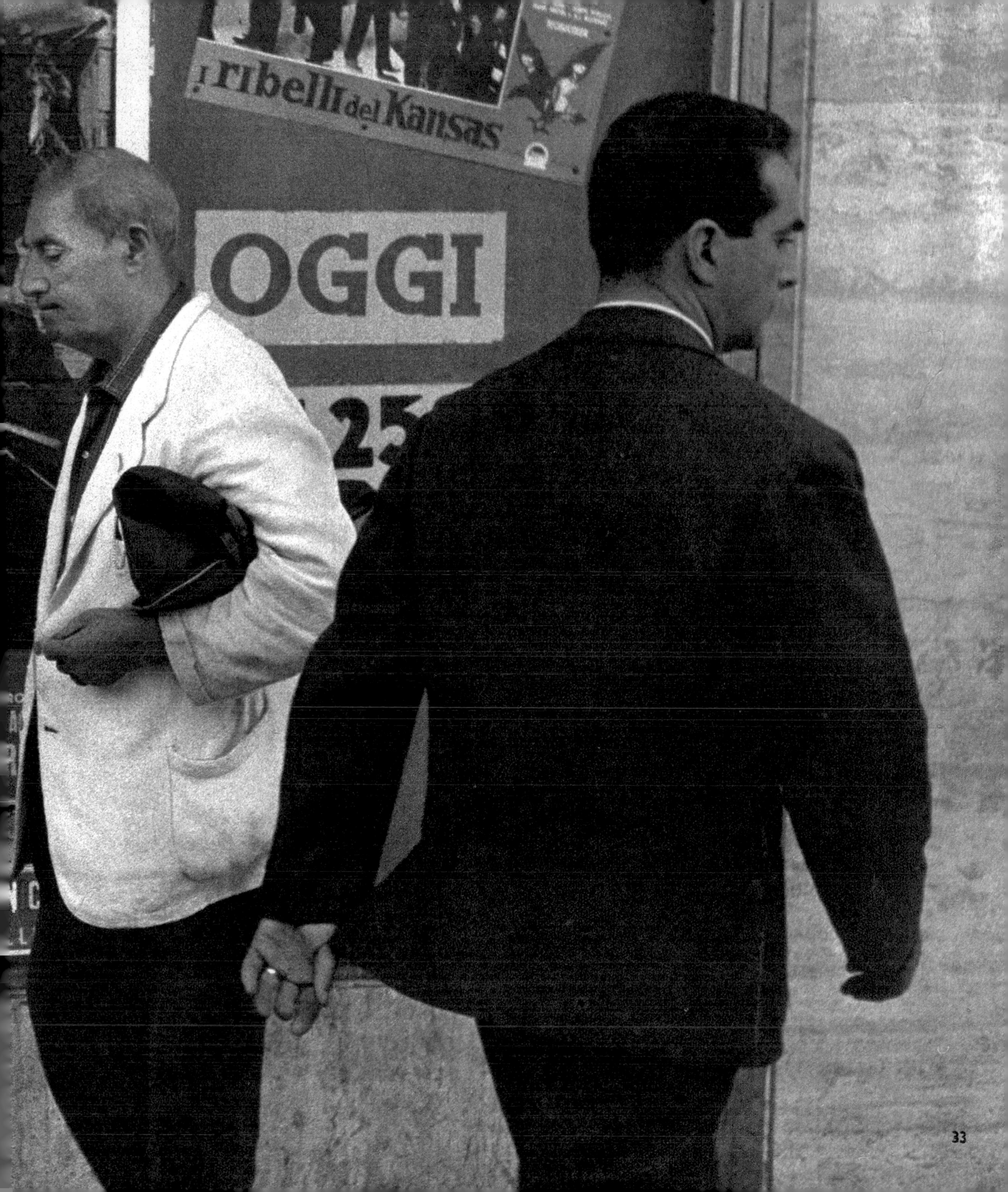

i ribelli del Kansas
OGGI

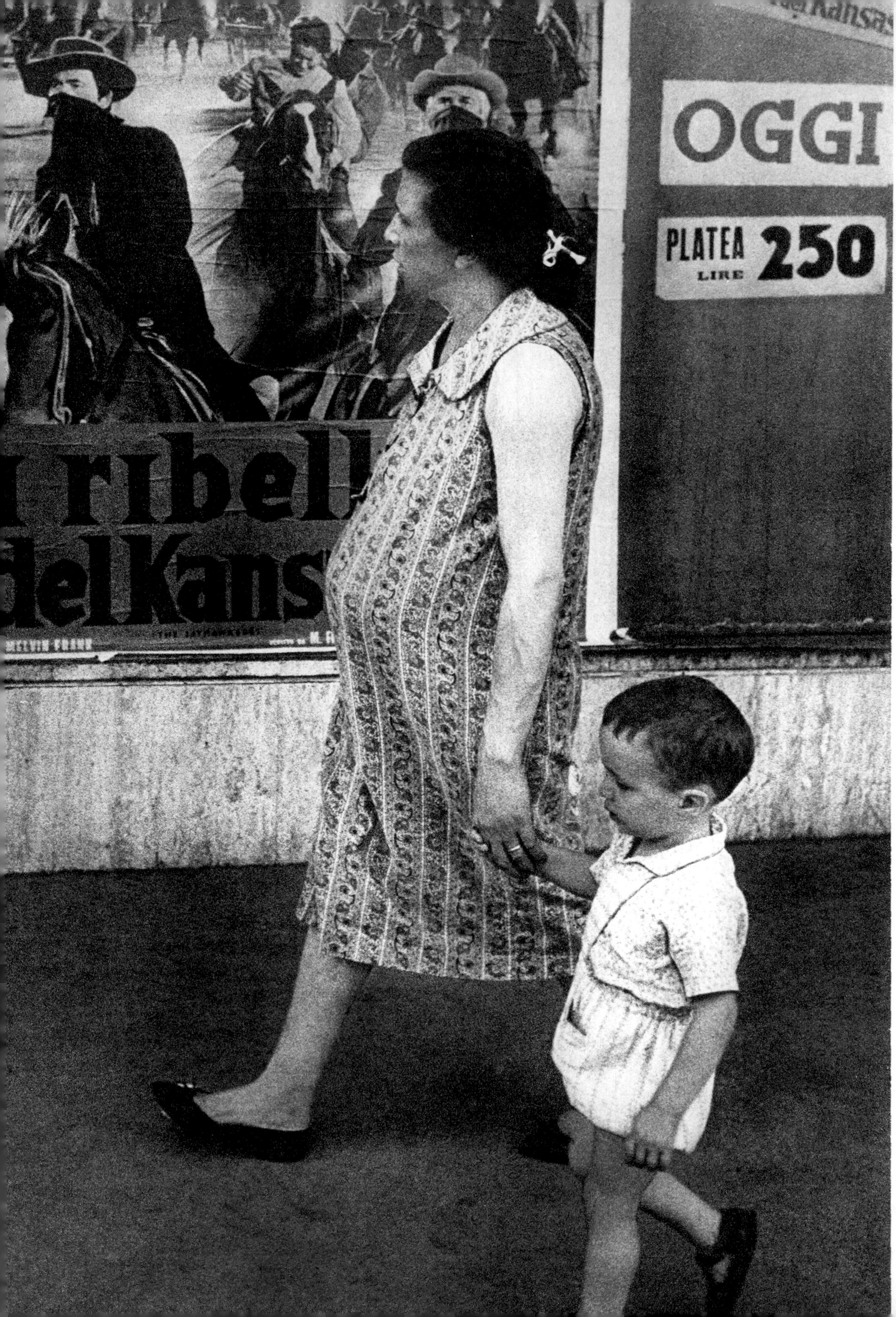
OGGI
PLATEA LIRE 250
ribell
delKans
MELVIN FRANK

47

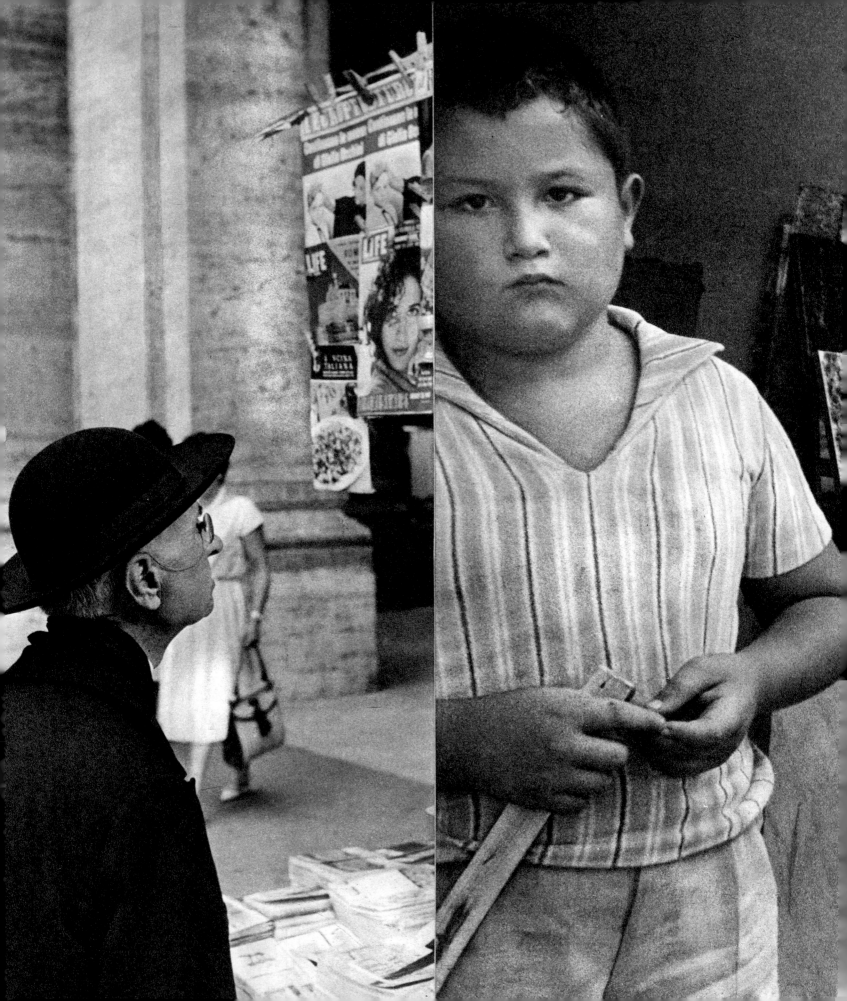

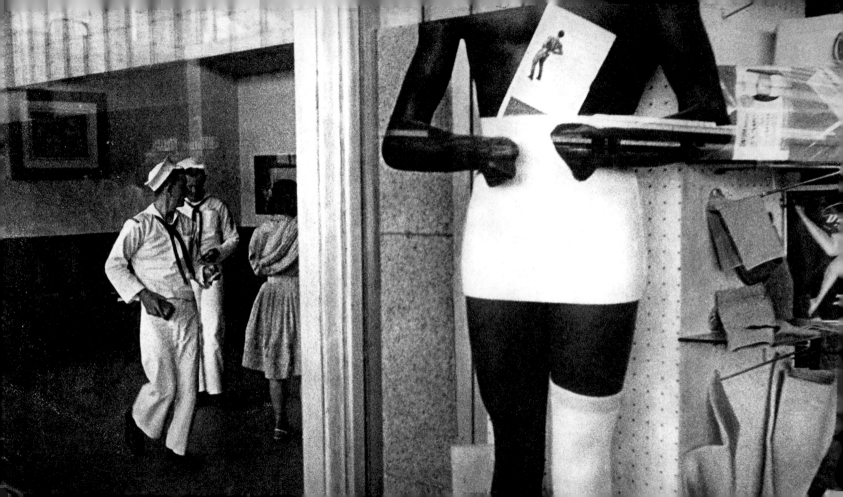

81

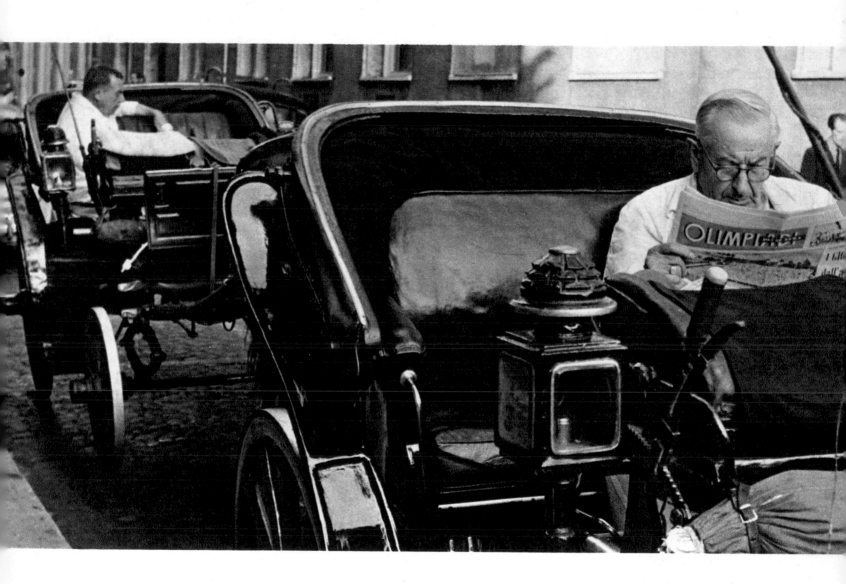

206-U
ALTO
CLASSIFICA FINALE
1 SAVLAKADZE URS 2,16
2 BRUMEL URS 2,16
3 THOMAS USA 2,14
4 BOLSHOV URS 2,14
5 PETTERSSON SVE 2,09
6 DUMAS USA 2,03

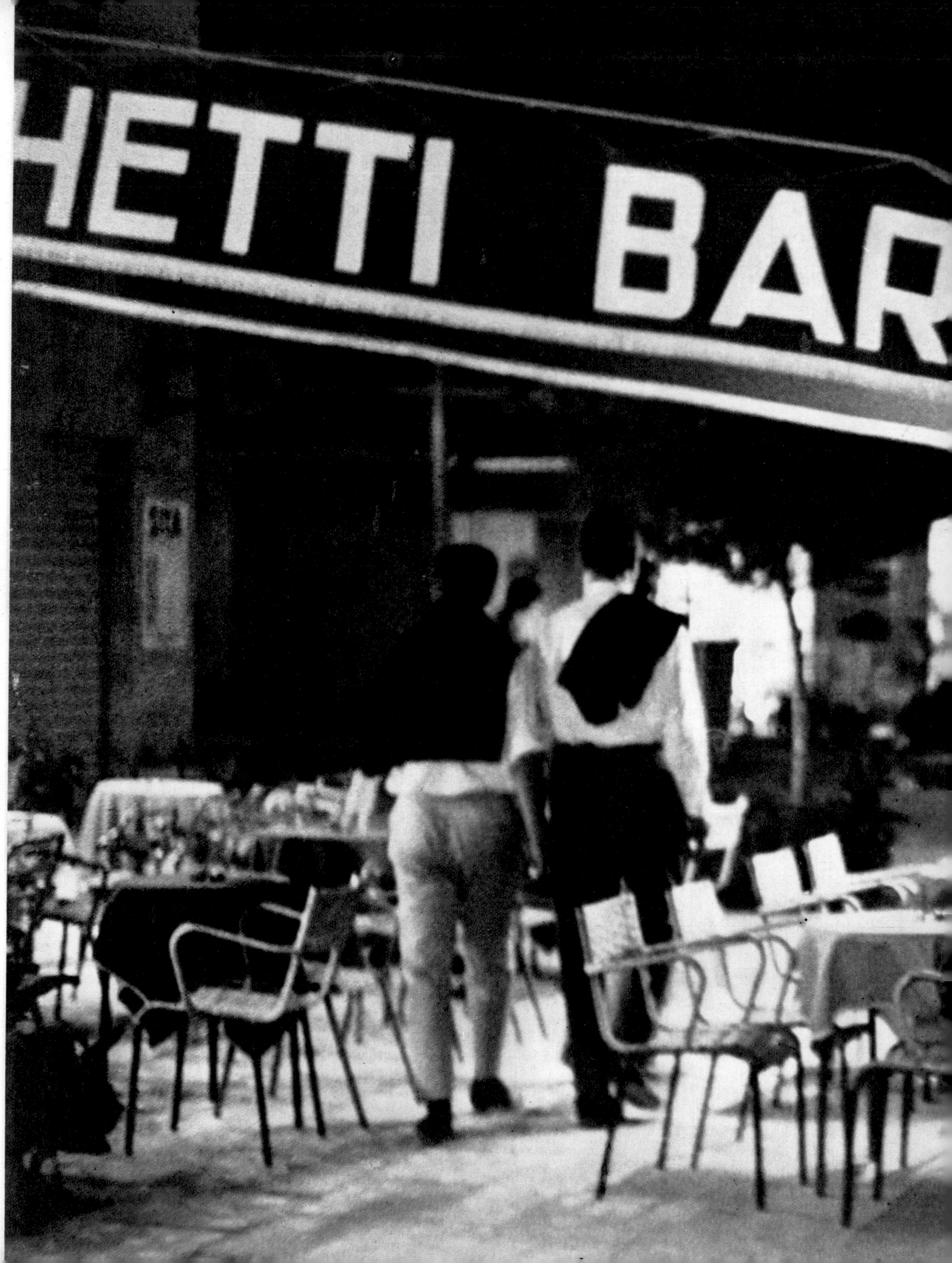
HETTI BAR